Tactical Bible Stories
Personal Security Tips from the Bible

By Rob Robideau

Table of Contents

Acknowledgements

To my Lord and Saviour Jesus Christ, you deserve all the honor and glory.

To my wonderful wife, Grace, thanks for encouraging me and being a sounding board through this project.

To my parents: Mom, thanks for helping with the proofreading and editing and Dad, for the advice and opinions.

To all the early reviewers, thank you for taking the time to check the book out before publishing to make sure I don't look like an idiot.

To those that have taken the time to share their thoughts and ideas with me on this subject via phone calls, books, preaching, blog posts, or podcasts, you all have helped to shape the way that I look at personal security. Thank you.

Introduction

Tactical Bible Stories is about the steps that you can take to protect and preserve life. It's not about the importance of self-defense and preserving life. That should already be settled in your mind before you pick up this book. We are going to talk about what comes next and actions you need to take.

In this book, we will outline the most critical personal security concepts and illustrate them with Bible stories to make them fun and easy for anyone to understand, apply, and remember.

We see from Bible stories that these concepts, ideas, and practices have been around since the beginning of time. They are tested, proven, and still used today with good reason. The next few pages are not going to blow your mind with amazing new ideas and tactics, but we will have fun approaching these timeless and essential concepts from a fresh new angle.

These critical and basic security concepts have been compiled based on my personal experience living in Nepal and from numerous hours spent with self-defense experts who have many years of experience studying, teaching, and writing about the dynamics of interpersonal conflict.

Despite the fantastic body of work already written about this subject, *Tactical Bible Stories* was written for the readers that may not be a part of the typical "self-defense circles". They may never have heard of Col. Jeff Cooper, Massad Ayoob, or Michael Janich, but they still recognize the importance of good personal security.

Tactical Bible Stories is not meant to become "the" book about personal security. The goal is to bring a new perspective that I hope will allow these critical concepts to reach a new group of people that might not have the tendency to pick up other commentaries on the subject of personal security.

I hope this book finds its way into the hands of people who aren't the typical students of self-defense. I want the ideas on these pages to help mothers, fathers, young men, and young ladies who aren't martial arts experts or firearm enthusiasts. I hope it can be taught by preachers, Sunday School teachers, and parents.

If properly applied, these practical safety measures can save lives and make you safer.

Preparation

"The horse is prepared against the day of battle: but safety is of the LORD." Proverbs 21:31

As believers, we understand that ultimately, safety comes from the Lord, but that doesn't mean that personal preparation or personal security is useless. It is foolish to expect God to perform a miracle to get you out of a problematic situation that could have been prevented with a little common sense or preparation.

Whenever we see miracles in Scripture, they aren't to rescue the stupid or ill prepared. After we as humans have done all that we can do, God steps in to make up the difference.

Preparation and trusting the Lord go hand in hand. They don't oppose each other. Preparation is about doing what we already know and are able to do, not taking God out of the equation and relying only on ourselves. Just because a person prepares for unwanted situations doesn't mean that they aren't trusting God to take care of them.

As parents, we have no problem helping our children and it's precious to see that they trust us to take care of them, but wouldn't you rather see your child learn how to avoid trouble and limit the situations where your intervention is necessary? God's Word gives us instructions and examples to follow so that we can grow and learn to properly handle difficult situations.

There are many factors in a violent confrontation that are out of our control, but that does not mean we shouldn't prepare for the parts that we might be able to control. Do what you can before you expect God to intervene on your behalf.

Proverbs 21:31(above) doesn't say that we shouldn't prepare the horse. It would be foolish to go into battle unprepared, but it also reminds us that our preparation alone can never guarantee our safety.

Nobody likes to talk about it, but no matter how much you prepare, there is still no guarantee of success. This can be a frustrating revelation. We want some sort of guarantee. We want insurance with a low deductible. We don't want the inevitable risk and uncertainty that comes with life.

Unfortunately, many people look at this and give up. They say, "If there is no guarantee of safety, why should I bother?"

They forget that there is risk involved in almost every aspect of life. Driving a car is a relatively dangerous proposition. Sure, you could purchase a horse and buggy and take up with the Amish, but most of us will just opt to take sensible measures to limit our risks. We wear safety belts. We make sure our cars are in proper working order. We pay attention while driving. These steps can end up saving our lives, but they still don't guarantee safety. They merely limit our exposure to danger in various situations.

Preparation is about limiting our exposure to danger in various situations. We can't prepare for everything, but preparation is still an essential part of personal security. The majority of the material covered in this book addresses the actions that you can take to prepare before an incident ever occurs. Let's get started!

Forethought

"But Daniel purposed in his heart that he would not defile himself..."
Daniel 1:8

Mental preparation and forethought are critical components of good personal security. Mentally walk yourself through possible situations and decide what you would do if they were to actually come to pass. Ask yourself, "If somebody steps up to my car window and threatens me with a gun, what will I do? If somebody starts walking directly toward me in a dark alley, what will I do? If somebody is loitering around my car in a dark parking lot, what will I do? If that ferocious, snarling dog manages to get over or under that fence, what will I do?"

It's important that we think through these situations in advance so that we don't have to make these decisions in the moment of conflict or trouble. When you force yourself to make instant decisions, it's very likely that you won't be thinking very clearly and you may not have all the best information available. In that moment, you won't be able to consult with your martial arts instructor or the teacher from your last handgun class. You won't be able to phone your boss and ask how the outcome of the decision would affect your employment. You have to think of these questions and considerations in advance so that you will make the right decision in the moment of conflict.

This concept applies to many areas of life. Personally, I made the decision not to make instant decisions unless absolutely necessary. I want the time to research things for myself so I can make the best choice. If a telemarketer calls with a fantastic deal, I refuse to make a decision at that instant, on that call. If the deal requires an instant decision, I miss the opportunity. Why? Because I believe it's important to have as much information as possible when making decisions. Decisions should not be made under stress or duress unless absolutely necessary.

If you believe that you hold in your mind all the information necessary to correctly and instantaneously execute 100% of the decisions that may be thrust upon you, you think too highly of yourself. There will be surprise decisions that you will be forced to make quickly, but shouldn't we limit those as much as possible? This is especially true when they concern the safety and security of ourselves and our loved ones!

It is not just about the availability of information. It is also about the fact that simple stress can mess up our decision making processes. Some people cannot even make good decisions in the presence of good friends because of the social stress involved. What about when you have the stress of the threat of the loss of life or limb hanging over your head? The decisions get far more difficult!

One of the first examples of the importance of forethought is seen with Eve and the serpent in the Garden of Eden. When the serpent came and talked with Eve, she knew what God had said about the tree, but she introduced her own ambiguity. Eve's quote wasn't exactly what God had said. God told Adam in *Genesis 2:17, "But of the tree of the knowledge of good and evil, thou shalt not eat of it: for in the day that thou eatest thereof thou shalt surely die."* Yet Eve said in Genesis 3:3, *"God hath said, Ye shall not eat of it, neither shall ye touch it, lest ye die."* God said nothing about touching the fruit. That was introduced by Eve in her spur of the moment protest. She did not have a thought out response to counter serious temptation. She was not mentally prepared.

She had all the necessary information in her head, but when she encountered that moment of temptation, she didn't know what to say. The stress of the confrontation caused hesitation and uncertainty, and eventually she acquiesced.

She encountered something outside her accepted routine and it created a new decision for her. The serpent introduced her to a situation that she did not anticipate. In her mind, she knew not to eat the fruit of the tree, but she hadn't planned on someone telling her how wonderful the tree was or attempting to contradict what she believed to be true.

This might have been avoided if Eve had thought through possible scenarios in advance. Even making simple mental decisions to only believe God's Word or to never eat the fruit would have been helpful in her situation.

Some might wonder, "How could she have possibly seen this coming? How could she have known to prepare herself mentally for this situation?" People ask similar questions today: "How can I think of these possible situations in advance?" I believe that we have a bit of an advantage over Eve. If you pick up a newspaper, turn on a TV, or listen to the radio, you will see that we live in a society filled with evil people that are capable of doing terrible things. Christians, of all people, should recognize this. We know that we are all sinners. We know that we are born with a sin nature and that even the best people are capable of breaking God's law in terrible and horrific ways.

Adam and Eve were given a specific mandate. Do not eat the fruit of the forbidden tree. Wherever some people have noble or good goals, there are always other people who want to ruin those plans, often for no logical reason. This is often a difficult concept for optimists or the uninitiated to grasp, but it is nonetheless true. We have to prepare to deal with these threats. We need to look into the future and attempt to see what undesirable decisions may be cast upon us.

Ambiguity is dangerous. Get as specific as possible. Eve probably took it upon herself not to touch the fruit of the forbidden tree so that she would not be tempted to eat the fruit. Being extra careful is not a bad idea.

Putting more space between you and the possible unwanted outcome is smart. In Eve's case, not thinking through the possible situations in advance made her decision unnecessarily complicated.

If you are going to err on the side of safety, do so in a precise and deliberate way. Decide that you will not touch the tree because it might lead to eating the fruit. Since not touching the fruit is only a secondary goal, figure out what situations would warrant it. When would you be willing to drop that buffer zone? What if you needed to trim the tree? What if you needed to break off some branches for a fire to stay warm? Are there any situations that would warrant touching the tree? The key is to think through the hypothetical situations so that you don't have to make decisions in the spur of the moment when you probably will not be thinking most clearly and may not have all the best information.

How do you come up with these hypothetical situations? Where can you start? Start general. Think of how your potential threats would begin and start making your decisions there. Choose scenarios that are most likely first. Don't spend all your time wondering about how you would fend off an alien invasion from above, zombies with rocket launchers, or an attacking lion that lives on a different continent. Your time would be better spent envisioning scenarios that could or would occur in your daily routine. Look at things that have happened in your local area or situations that you worry about. Forethought requires no monetary investment, and only a minimal time investment. You can work through many situations in a relatively short amount of time, so be thorough. Try to think of everything.

When you mentally build your hypothetical situations, try to make them as realistic as possible. Include as many details as you can. This will serve two purposes. First, the extra details will help the scenario to seem more realistic in your head. When you can inject more detail into the visualization of these scenarios, it is more likely that you will recognize and respond quickly if they actually come to pass.

Second, the extra details will help you inject realism into the assessment of your decisions and their outcomes. Don't just imagine a bad guy, imagine a screaming, heavy-set male attacker with a knife in his right hand, moving quickly with a crazy glint in his eyes and wearing a leather jacket. What tools? What clothes? What size? What disposition? All of these factors can change how you should respond. How can you properly assess your decision without these details?

When you make a decision, try to figure out what would happen next. Would my knife really cut through that leather jacket? Would I really be able to get the knife out in time? Would I be able to draw a firearm and shoot a moving target if he is already within fifteen feet? Could I outrun him? Carry your decision to its logical conclusion and if it is unsatisfactory, go back and do something else.

Keep adjusting your decision until you are satisfied with the conclusion of your mental reenactment. Be as realistic as possible. When in doubt, err on the side of safety by underestimating your skill, speed, dexterity, memory, accuracy, etc. If you find a reason that a given tactic would not work, go back and try again in a different way.

With some scenarios, it may not be possible to come up with a "happy ending." In those cases, figure out what will give you the best possible outcome. These are some of the most important decisions to make in advance, because they are the most difficult to make under stress.

If things change, go back and reevaluate those decisions. If your skill level changes because you aren't able to get to the range for practice, you should reevaluate some of your decisions. If you sprain your ankle, you might need to change a few decisions. If you get married or have a child, go back and take another look at those decisions. If you learn a new skill or use a new tool, you might alter your tactics in certain situations.

If you discover new information, you should also reevaluate. Maybe you just realized how difficult it can be to cut a leather coat. You may need to rethink the situations where you planned on using a knife. Maybe you did some ballistics experiments with your .380 ACP handgun and found out that it was not as powerful as you thought. You might want to rethink your tactics with that tool.

Do not be afraid of new or contradictory information. Welcome it as an opportunity to double check your decisions. Don't be afraid to ask for the opinions of others when planning for these situations. Another person may see a variable in your scenario that you missed.

Never underestimate the value of a fresh outlook. Get input from spouses and even children. See what your coworkers would do in your work related scenarios. Listen to the suggestions. Don't let your ego get in the way. You don't want to make mistakes with lives on the line.

Daniel was a positive Bible example of forethought:

Daniel 1:8 "But Daniel purposed in his heart that he would not defile himself with the portion of the king's meat, nor with the wine which he drank: therefore he requested of the prince of the eunuchs that he might not defile himself."

Daniel was in a situation that was far more difficult than yours or mine. He was a captured prisoner in an enemy nation. Everything was new and foreign. Everything was intimidating. He constantly made decisions that could mean life or death. He was a young person who was just forming his ideas and opinions of the world and people around him.

In this difficult situation, he realized the importance of forethought and making decisions in advance. He knew that if he could anticipate and prepare for potentially difficult situations, he had a better chance of a positive outcome. He had not yet been asked to defile himself with the king's meat, but he saw this possibility in his mind and made the appropriate decision beforehand. He even took action before the potential conflict.

His forethought served him well throughout his life. Later, we see that other leaders were plotting to kill Daniel and remove him from power with absurd laws that did not allow him to petition God. When these laws would have presented most believers with a moral dilemma, Daniel knew exactly what he was going to do without protest or drama. He openly petitioned God as he had every day prior. The newly minted laws presented no moral quandary for Daniel because he knew who he relied upon and had decided to be faithful to his God. We know from the rest of the story that God was just as faithful to Daniel in the lion's den.

If Daniel had waited to make these decisions when confronted, the story could have ended very differently. Daniel might have backed down and become a part of the heathen society. He probably wouldn't have had the amazing testimony that led his captor the king to proclaim the one, true God throughout his kingdom.

Forethought and making decisions in advance can keep us from making potentially devastating bad choices and is an essential component of preparation and personal security.

Training

"And when Abram heard that his brother was taken captive, he armed his trained servants... and pursued them..." Genesis 14:14

Mental preparation alone is not enough if we want to respond properly to threats. Training is also critical. The reasoning behind training is similar to the argument for mental preparation: Our minds and bodies learn much faster when information is presented and processed in advance, rather than learning through trial and error.

The Bible does not say exactly how Abraham's servants were trained. Were they trained as soldiers? As bodyguards? Did they learn tactics? We don't know. We can assume that they were trained in the use of weapons as this verse says they were being armed for pursuit.

The point is that Abraham thought it was important to prepare and train for possible problems. He knew that training would give them a necessary advantage. When that kidnapping occurred, his servants weren't just beginning to figure out which end of the sword went into the other guy. They were trained and ready.

The first time you run should not be when you are chased by a violent criminal. The first time you draw a handgun should not be when your life depends on it. The first time you throw a punch (or take a punch) should not be in a street fight. That's not the time to be learning. That is when we should be executing decisive, practiced movements for the umpteen millionth time.

When we see a child step up to home plate with a bat for the first time ever, we understand that their performance will not be the same as after a year of little league games and practice. We expect them to under-perform. We know there will be a learning curve.

Before the boy in little league is put in the batter's box for the first time, Dad probably spent hours showing his son how to hold and swing the bat. He was probably instructed on how to watch and follow the ball. He spent hours and hours training for his first at-bat so that he can make a good showing and the only thing really at stake is the father's pride. How much more important is practice and training when safety is on the line?

If we pit an inexperienced shooter against a professional competitive shooter or defensive instructor who spends numerous hours on the range each week, we know who will come out on top. If we have two men equal in every other way, but one is trained in the martial arts and the other has never fought with his hands, we have a pretty good idea how that fight will go. Our actions will be quicker and more decisive when we have trained properly.

It is not a good idea to introduce our minds and bodies to brand new decisions, actions, and motions during life or death situations. We should learn the most effective techniques and train in advance so that we can perform them flawlessly under pressure. Training helps to make sure that your learning *curve* does not turn into a *straight line*!

An alternative to training is just figuring it out on your own. While technically "figuring it out" is still training, using proper training tools and methods will speed up the learning process in an amazing way and keep you from getting frustrated at slow progress. Proper training saves an immense amount of time and often helps you to master concepts, tools, and techniques that you could not have figured out on your own.

Training can be as simple as reading a book or as complicated as traveling to and working with a specialized trainer in a multi-day course. If you lack the time or financial resources to attend classes, do what you can. Make the best use of the resources that you have.

One of the simplest and least expensive ways to train is on your own using a quality training book or video. Good authors can explain difficult concepts in a way that even a simpleton like myself can understand. Many also use good photos to illustrate the concepts.

Don't just take the information in. That isn't enough. To properly train yourself, you have to actually go through the motions. You have to build what many people call muscle memory (we know that muscles don't actually have memory). Read until you understand the concept, then train until you can actually perform it. Some of this can be done at home with a training gun, but some of this has to be done with live fire.

Take your training to the next level with a friend. It's difficult to get feedback when you are training on your own. Even watching yourself in the mirror doesn't always work because it can mess up the skill that you are focusing on. Invite a friend over and explain what you are doing. It's even better if it's a friend that also wants to train. They will be motivated to learn the concepts just as well as you and will offer more intelligent critical advice. Have them watch you and look for errors. There are often things that you don't realize you are doing that are very obvious to someone who is watching you.

Make sure you have the right attitude concerning criticism. Good criticism is necessary to become better at any learned skill. Self-criticism or criticism from another party will help us find the areas we need to work on and correct. When you get a piece of criticism that might be a little hard to swallow, remember that it's only to make you better.

If you don't have a friend or don't feel like bothering your friends, you can set up a camera to record you. Most cellphones or point and shoot cameras have video modes that will be sufficient. Set it on a countertop at home or a nearby table at the range. You don't need to record yourself in HD with studio lighting to see that your elbow flaps wide like a chicken during your draw. If you feel particularly adventurous, post your videos online and ask for criticism. Make sure you have thick skin!

Train with a good instructor. The best feedback comes from someone with a trained eye. A good instructor has helped numerous students and knows the most common mistakes to look for. They also have a better eye for the subtle mistakes that you or a friend may not notice. Sure, you can rely on your golf buddy to watch your swing and give you advice, but the golf pro knows what he's looking for and has lots of experience to back him up. Think of a good instructor like a golf pro for your shooting.

Most people end up using some combination of all three methods mentioned above. It would be quite expensive to keep a knowledgeable instructor on hand for every training session. Most people will read and study on their own, go to a class to ensure that they understand and get down the basics, then continue practicing and evaluating later with a friend or camera. Find whatever combination works for you.

Some people require more training than others. Background makes a difference. If your father was a professional airline pilot and you spent a lot of time in the cockpit with him as a child, pilot training will probably be a breeze and in some cases unnecessary. Likewise, if you grow up and learn proper firearm handling as a child, many of the basic concepts of using a firearm for self-defense will come easily.

Unfortunately, some backgrounds require more training because of bad habits or bad training in the past. There are a lot of people that think they know a lot about firearm handling, but end up scaring the instructors as they show off their special behind-the-back shooting tricks. Even if you think you know the basics, listen to the instructors and hear what they have to say.

Some tools require more training than others. Sometimes this is because the tool is complicated, but sometimes the simplest tools are most effectively used in a relatively complicated manner.

There is a point of diminishing return. There is such a thing as too much training. Doubling your training won't necessarily double your proficiency. Once you have learned how to properly and efficiently execute the basics, you move on to honing those skills, polishing the edge.

When you sharpen a dull blade, the biggest return on your time investment is the initial time spent with a coarse stone. You take the blade from a point where it is not cutting to a point where it is cutting. When you break out the finer stones and the strop, you can make it super sharp, but it's really only a little sharper than the result of your initial work.

Even though you will see the biggest payoff at the beginning of your training, don't stop there!

The many hours spent polishing your skills past what may be deemed "acceptable" by most of society are extremely important. The conflicts that we prepare for are not merely tests where achieving a minimum score assures success. These unforeseen violent encounters require that we outperform an unknown opponent with an unknown skill set and unknown proficiency. There is no such thing as being too proficient or too prepared for conflict.

Focus on your strengths in execution; focus on your weaknesses in training.

It's important to focus on training to your weaknesses. This requires realistic self-evaluation to find your weaknesses. When you find your weaknesses, it takes discipline to spend time focusing on what is probably the least pleasant and most difficult portion of your training. Unfortunately, violent encounters don't have rules and your opponent most definitely won't agree to avoid your weak areas. Training to your weak areas will give you the biggest "bang for your buck" when it comes to time and effort in training.

Remember that there are no rules in reality.

There are always limits to your training. Over-training or training too hard can be counter-productive. You don't want to train so hard that you injure yourself and make yourself more vulnerable. Most people don't have to worry about this, but you should evaluate your training to make sure that it makes you stronger and more prepared, not the opposite.

There are many rules at most gun ranges that are not imposed in real-life situations. These unrealistic rules and limitations don't mean that you should give up on training at the range, but you should constantly remind yourself of how it would really be in the real world.

If you do not remember your ultimate goals, your training will turn into an unrealistic sport. Most "martial" arts have gone this way. Sometimes it is because of social pressure to be more politically correct, but often the practitioners have forgotten their original goals and left reality. Remember the goal of your training so you can keep it as realistic as possible.

Training realistically is critical and unrealistic training is completely useless. A major league baseball player would probably have fun practicing with a little league team. It would probably feed his ego and make him feel like he is a fantastic player, but it does nothing to prepare him for the reality of what he will face in a major league baseball game.

Train with the tools you will actually have. It's fun to shoot the decked out battle rifles and play with nunchucks, but are you really likely to have them with you if you are attacked? If you are lucky enough to spend some time with a Dillon Mini-gun or a grenade launcher, good for you, but unless you find a way to conceal and carry them on your person, don't try to convince yourself that you are training realistically for a violent encounter.

Do not neglect hand-to-hand combat training for those times you won't have defensive tools. Unless you are extremely creative and willing to break many laws, you cannot carry defensive tools with you everywhere. Don't ignore those vulnerable times. Learn to use your hands to defend yourself. TSA can't take those away... yet.

Be creative in your training. Don't get stuck in a rut. Train for the various scenarios you envisioned during your mental preparation. As you train and gain skills, be sure to head back and run those mental scenarios again to see if there are new ways to handle certain situations.

Proverbs 22:26 says "Train up a child in the way he should go: and when he is old, he will not depart from it."

A little training goes a long way. Don't neglect this critical area of preparation!

Bear

"And he took his staff in his hand, and chose him five smooth stones out of the brook, and put them in a shepherd's bag which he had, even in a scrip; and his sling was in his hand: and he drew near to the Philistine." 1 Samuel 17:40

David was preparing for a violent confrontation: a one-on-one fight with an armed and dangerous giant. Here we have an experienced man of war against a young man of the wilderness who was unlearned in tactics, methods, and tools of war. David needed every advantage that he could muster. He needed the most effective tools of war that he could carry.

David had at his disposal, the most potent and deadly killing tools that were available at that time. He could have had the best sword manufactured by the finest craftsmen in the kingdom. If he wanted, he could have had the best bow and arrows on the battlefield. King Saul offered David his personal armor. David was the representative of the Israelite army and could have had any weapon he wanted.

And Saul armed David with his armour, and he put an helmet of brass upon his head; also he armed him with a coat of mail. And David girded his sword upon his armour, and he assayed to go; for he had not proved it. And David said unto Saul, I cannot go with these; for I have not proved them. And David put them off him. 1 Samuel 17:38-39

Despite having access to the most advanced tools of war that his nation could offer, David chose to use a sling, a staff, and stones.

Some might say that he chose these lesser weapons so that his victory would magnify the Lord, but I beg to differ. I believe David had faith in the promise of God, but he also wanted to make sure he had the tools that he would be able to wield most effectively in this dangerous battle.

In my opinion, David's sling was the equivalent of a modern day .22lr plinking pistol. David spent a great deal of time outdoors in the wilderness and more than likely, he had his sling and staff with him at all times. They were probably used on pests and predators and practiced with often. The sling and staff were the tools that David had become proficient and comfortable with.

He didn't want the super-cool weapons endorsed by the "Chris Costas" or "Travis Haleys" of the day. He didn't care what the king used or the other great war heroes. He wanted a tool that he knew he could wield with confidence and proficiency. He understood that a tool that he could not use effectively was useless to him.

Fortunately, most of us are not preparing for an immediate battle with a giant. When we choose our tools, we plan to train and familiarize ourselves with them, but we can still learn from David and his gear selection.

It is important that you select gear that is right for you. Do not select your defensive tools like a star-struck teenager selects basketball shoes: "These are the shoes my favorite athlete wears. I'm going to use these!" That's fine for a child who doesn't know any better, but we are talking about defending yourself, your family, and your home in the event of a violent encounter. Please use a little more sense.

Who doesn't want the same shoes that Michael Jordan wears? But what if your foot isn't the same shape and they don't fit? What if you play baseball (not basketball) and need cleats instead of basketball shoes?

Who wouldn't want to use King Saul's tools of war? I'm sure that many men on that battlefield would have killed for those prestigious weapons, but they didn't fit David. David didn't know how to use them effectively. David understood the importance of making sure his tools were right for him.

Your gear should be chosen based on your needs, not the needs of your local SWAT team or favorite special forces unit. This is not to say that you can't end up with the same gear that your local SWAT team uses. If you examine the situations where you would use a defensive tool, go shoot several guns, and find out that you ended up with the same gun as the SWAT team, good for you!

There are actually a number of good reasons that you might end up with some of the same gear as your local law enforcement officers. Maybe, after researching available firearms, you both came to the conclusion that gun X has superior reliability or minimal recoil or is easy to maintain and find parts for. Make sure the research is there. Mentally apply the tool to the possible scenarios and situations in which you would use a defensive tool to see if it will actually help you. You should be confident that it works with your lifestyle, family situation, clothing, work environment, local laws, skill level, training regimen, etc.

When the proper selection process is in place, you will end up with effective and realistic tools that will work for you.

If you want to buy knives, guns, or impact weapons because they are unusual, have historical significance, look cool, or make neat sounds, go ahead. Just don't try to convince yourself that you are choosing the most effective defensive tools. Those are toys. They are show pieces. They are marvels of modern technology and design, but unless you make sure that they fit you and your needs, they aren't the best defensive tools.

Your tools should be selected for practicality. Your tools should be chosen for usefulness. Your tools should be chosen because you know that you can use them effectively.

I always hated it when math teachers would require me to show my work, but they were making sure that there was a thought process behind the answer, rather than just copying or guessing. The math teacher wants you to be able to come up with the right answer every time. If a student guesses or copies another student, they have no idea whether or not they have the correct answer. I want you to know that you have the right tools because you used the right process to select them.

Unfortunately, gear gets far more attention than it really deserves and there are a number of reasons. Gear is where most companies make the majority of their money, so they spend lots of money on advertising to

29

make sure we know about and talk about their gear. We are materialistic human beings and we love stuff. Everybody loves to talk about the latest gadgets and it is easy to get fixated on gear. Please do not misunderstand me. Proper tools can greatly increase your effectiveness and potency, but they are only a small part of the overall picture. Your gear selection definitely needs to be addressed, but don't forget the other areas of preparation also.

You don't need the latest and greatest super-ti-shamium, high-speed, low-drag, gun endorsed by the hottest competition shooters. Your priority should be finding realistic tools that will help you prevail.

Awareness

"Therefore let us not sleep, as do others; but let us watch and be sober." I Thessalonians 5:6

Now that we have prepared ourselves both mentally and physically for a violent confrontation and have the proper gear, we need to give ourselves a chance to use that preparation. Awareness allows us to recognize untoward situations and apply our training and tactics.

Because of your mental preparation, you know what you would do in given situations, but now you have to be able to recognize those situations with enough time and space to react effectively. This recognition comes through awareness.

Without awareness, all your preparation is useless. Awareness is a critical link in the chain of personal security and if ignored, it doesn't matter how well you do everything else. The chain will be broken because of this weak link.

Without awareness, you won't be able to use your awesome gun fighting skills. You won't be able to execute your well thought-out plan. You won't be able to deploy your well-chosen defensive tool. You have to be aware in order to spot the trouble in time to deal with it.

Unless you are in a coma, you are somewhat aware of what is happening around you, but we are talking about taking it to the next level. We are talking about awareness that will help you maintain your personal security and this requires conscious effort.

Everyone has ears, but not everybody is listening.

Even if they are listening, what are they doing with that information? Are they ignoring it, or are they comparing it to their database of information and previous experience to look for trouble?

The key to awareness is examining reality in such a way that you can compare and match it to the situations you have already prepared for mentally.

While no one thinks that they are "unaware" of their surroundings, everyone should be willing to admit that they can increase their awareness in some way. Awareness is absolutely essential to your personal security. Let's take look at two ways for you to step up your awareness.

Mindset

"So he brought down the people unto the water: and the LORD said unto Gideon, Every one that lappeth of the water with his tongue, as a dog lappeth, him shalt thou set by himself; likewise every one that boweth down upon his knees to drink. And the number of them that lapped, putting their hand to their mouth, were three hundred men: but all the rest of the people bowed down upon their knees to drink water. And the LORD said unto Gideon, By the three hundred men that lapped will I save you, and deliver the Midianites into thine hand: and let all the other people go every man unto his place." Judges 7:5-7

33

In this passage we have Gideon putting together an army to go against an enemy so large that they were practically innumerable. The Lord has decided that Gideon's army is too large and comes up with a test to send men home and narrow it down to the best of the best.

Gideon brought his ten thousand men down to the river and watched them as they drank. The Lord told Gideon to separate the men based on how they drank from the river. The vast majority of the army got down on their knees and put their face to the water to drink. Three percent of the men did something different. They squatted down to the water, dipped their hand in the water like a ladle, and brought the water up to their mouth to drink.

The Lord told Gideon to send home all the men that got down on their knees to drink and those who put their faces to the water to lap like a dog. Those men put themselves in a position of vulnerability by getting on their knees. By putting their faces in the water, they severely limited their awareness because they could not see what was happening around them. These are not smart moves, especially with a large and powerful enemy nearby. The men that got down on their knees and put their faces in the water in a time of war were fools.

Unfortunately, many people walk through life with the equivalent of their faces stuck in the water. They constantly make decisions that restrict their awareness and decrease their personal security.

Gideon needed men that had a mindset of awareness. He needed men that were aware of their surroundings at all times and were constantly paying attention. The men that stayed on their feet and kept looking around while drinking were the men that the Lord knew Gideon needed.

Gideon could have just asked the men, "How many of you don't pay attention all the time?", but he probably wouldn't have gotten much of a response. I am quite certain that most of the men considered themselves to be very aware of their surroundings. They didn't think they were being unsafe. They didn't see their own shortcomings in the area of awareness.

The test that the Lord gave Gideon did more than just ask if the men had a mindset of awareness. It showed Gideon how much they valued awareness. When these men came to the water to drink, they made a quick exception in their mind. They said, "Nothing is going to happen for a moment. I'll stick my face in the water and save a little time." There was no doubt that they were getting the fastest drink. There was no doubt that this was the easiest way to drink. They thought this was a reasonable risk. They thought that a little extra speed and convenience was worth the small risk of ambush during those few seconds.

The Lord considered this moment of ignorance to be an unacceptable risk. He wanted Gideon's men to be aware at all times. He wanted men that didn't take unnecessary risks for convenience. He wanted men that had a mindset of awareness.

Awareness isn't something that you turn on and off. It's a mindset and the Lord was looking for men that placed enough emphasis on awareness that they didn't make exceptions, especially unconscious exceptions. These unconscious exceptions can be much more dangerous than our conscious decisions to become unaware. It is sometimes acceptable to look at a circumstance and weigh the pros and cons before you decide to do something that may impair your awareness. Once you make sure all the doors and windows are closed and locked, the security system is on, the motion sensor lights are on, and the dog is ready to bark at intruders, it is probably OK to close your eyes and get some rest. It's a calculated risk. You took action to limit the risk and determined that your rest was worth it.

35

The dangerous part is when you don't even consider the security risks involved in limiting your awareness. You just decided that you were tired, so you went to sleep. You didn't think about the security risks, you were solely focused on your convenience.

Unfortunately, this is how most people live their lives. They are more concerned about speed, convenience, and entertainment than their security. They have made lifestyle decisions that cause them to constantly accept unnecessary and live life oblivious to their surroundings.

They have decided that the entertainment value of their iPod and ear buds is worth not being able to hear what is going on around them. They have decided that the security of a table where you can sit with your back to the wall is not worth the inconvenience of the wait. Whether or not they know it, they have a mindset that values convenience over the awareness that is necessary for good personal security.

In the story of Gideon's men, drinking from cupped hands was not the convenient way to drink. It probably took longer to get a good drink. It would have been much faster and easier to stick your face in the water and gulp it up, but they had a mindset that valued awareness over convenience.

How can you develop that mindset of awareness? How can you stop making unconscious decisions that degrade your awareness and personal security? How can you increase your awareness?

Setting and maintaining a high level of awareness requires constant self-evaluation. First, look at your lifestyle and see if there are any decisions that you are regularly making that restrict your awareness. Are these decisions worth it? If not, make some changes so that your decisions properly reflect your concern for good personal security.

You should constantly be asking yourself, "Am I at an optimum level of awareness?" If not, ask yourself, "What can I do to get there?"

At first, you will need to figure out ways to remind yourself. Put a note on your dashboard to remind you to look around before you unlock the doors and get out of the car. Put a note by the door where you exit your home. Set a few alarms on your phone as you are getting started in this process. Have a spouse or friend help remind you. Be creative and find your own ways to constantly remind yourself to increase your awareness.

Once you get started with monitoring your awareness and examining your decisions based on how they affect your awareness, it builds on itself like a snowball rolling downhill. You will develop that all-important mindset of awareness and you won't even have to think about it.

It will probably take some time to adjust your mentality and raise your overall awareness, but be patient. With constant self-monitoring, your awareness will improve noticeably. Remember that there is no finish line with developing awareness. You will never completely "arrive". It should be a constant journey of increasing awareness.

Remember that no one ever reaches the ultimate level of awareness where they know everything that is happening around them. Everyone gets caught off guard every once in a while, but if you start evaluating yourself and making good decisions, you will have a much higher level of awareness that will give you more options when trouble comes.

Differentiators

And the Gileadites took the passages of Jordan before the Ephraimites: and it was so, that when those Ephraimites which were escaped said, Let me go over; that the men of Gilead said unto him, Art thou an Ephraimite? If he said, Nay; Then said they unto him, Say now Shibboleth: and he said Sibboleth: for he could not frame to pronounce it right. Then they took him, and slew him at the passages of Jordan: and there fell at that time of the Ephraimites forty and two thousand. Judges 12:5-6

In this passage, the people of Gilead needed a way to tell who the "bad guys" were. Their looks and cultures were very similar in many ways, but the Gileadites found a differentiator to tell the Ephraimites apart. They spoke differently. There was a specific word that they couldn't pronounce properly. The Ephraimites could not pronounce the "sh" sound in "shibboleth".

In Nepal, there are several variations on the English "t" sound. As a foreigner, it is very difficult for me to hear the differences between these sounds and pronounce them myself. It requires slightly different placement of the tongue for more or less air. These are subtle differences that I haven't picked up on yet.

Because of my unfamiliarity with the details of the language, I will pronounce certain words improperly or with an obvious "accent". They sound perfect to me, but locals just look at me like I spoke to them in Klingon. "Shibboleth" was one of the words that the Gileadites knew foreigners had trouble with.

The Gileadites used the pronunciation of this word as a test to see if a person was a threat. This test helped them to tell if an unknown person was a friend or an enemy. When they were approached by a new person, they knew exactly what they were looking for: "How do they pronounce this word?"

Knowing what they were looking for helped them to spot threats that they might have missed otherwise.

They could have looked at facial features. They could have asked questions about obscure local knowledge. They could have looked at clothing or weapons. They could have used many things, but they looked at their personal experience and found a differentiator that they could focus on to recognize threats.

Just being aware isn't enough. You have to know what you are looking for. The Gileadites could have easily stood watch over the bridges and still let the Ephraimites pass unobstructed if they didn't know what they were looking for. Instead, they looked analytically at their surroundings and the details, spotted an important difference, and used that observation to their advantage.

These differences in the details will warn you. If you are paying attention to the details, you will notice when things change.

Not all changes indicate danger, but almost all danger is preceded by some sort of warning signal. These warning signals are normally small and often go unnoticed, but if you are paying attention, they can be as obvious as a screaming siren.

The Gileadites found this differentiator because they were paying attention to the details of their surroundings and they knew what to look for. They spent plenty of time around their fellow countrymen and knew exactly how they pronounced the word "shibboleth". When they heard the Ephraimites pronounce it differently, they picked up on that.

Did that differentiator work 100% of the time? Probably not. There were probably a few people who could pronounce it properly, but the majority of the time, it properly identified their threats.

You might be able to find a word that criminals have a hard time saying, but that isn't the point. The lesson we need to take away is that we need to find differentiators that we can use to recognize threats. What will you be looking for? Hidden faces? People standing in the shadows? Hidden hands? Furtive glances at security cameras? Find your own differentiators.

Unfortunately, criminals don't walk around with signs that say, "Look out! I'm going to rob/harm you!" You have to look for the signs. You have to come up with your "shibboleth" to look for.

6th Sense

"When she had heard of Jesus, came in the press behind, and touched his garment. For she said, If I may touch but his clothes, I shall be whole. And straightway the fountain of her blood was dried up; And she felt in her body that she was healed of that plague. And Jesus, immediately knowing in himself that virtue had gone out of him, turned him about in the press, and said, Who touched my clothes? And his disciples said unto him, Thou seest the multitude thronging thee, and sayest thou, Who touched me? And he looked round about to see her that had done this thing." Mar 5:27-32

Most of the time when we spot something that isn't right, we don't immediately know exactly what is wrong. We just know that something doesn't fit. Something is out of place and it bothers us. It could be a smell, a facial expression, tone of voice, or any number of seemingly insignificant indicators that alert us.

Some people call it the "sixth sense". It is our ability to spot something wrong without specifically attributing that sense to our hearing, sight, feel, taste, or smell. Maybe it was ESP!?! In reality, the answer is much simpler and rather boring. Our "sixth sense" is actually a subliminal combination of all of our God-given senses. It is when we notice things without purposefully noticing.

But what allows us to do this? What gives us that reference? Knowing what is right. Knowing what is correct. Knowing how things should be (and knowing them well) allows us to spot small deviations from the norm.

When dealing with cash, you will never be able to anticipate, learn, and look for all the errant details that could be on every counterfeit piece. You have to study real money and know it so well that any deviation, no matter how small, will stand out.

Likewise, the infinite variations in which trouble can present itself mean that all the studying and advance preparation in the world cannot prepare us for every possible problem. We have to become students of all that is right around us. We need to become so "in tune" with our surroundings and what is normal, that we can instantly recognize anything that is amiss.

Soon after we first moved to Nepal, I headed out to school on a beautiful day. It's about a 25 minute trip on my scooter and other than unusually light traffic, I didn't really notice anything out of the ordinary. When I reached the school, I discovered that the gates were closed and locked, so I called a friend and asked what was going on. He let me know that the roads were empty and stores were shut down because of the threats of violence of a major political party. As I carefully made my way home, I noticed the people looking at me peculiarly, children playing cricket in the streets, and many closed shops. I noticed that all the vehicles I was passing were marked journalist, medical, or official vehicles.

I continued blissfully unaware into a dangerous situation for so long because I was not familiar enough with my surroundings to recognize that things were different. I had not been paying enough attention. I had only lived here for a short time. I can make lots of good excuses, but basically, I was a bumbling idiot and I wasn't paying enough attention to my surroundings.

Now that I have lived here for some time, and paid more attention to my surroundings, I quickly recognize the warning signs and get back home and off the roads right away. The warning signs are there every time, but if we don't have a reference to compare them to, they don't help.

With increased awareness and an acute knowledge of your surroundings, you don't need flashing neon lights or angry villagers yelling and chasing you with torches and pitchforks in order to figure out that something is wrong. You can spot trouble by the subtle, sometimes subliminal changes in your surroundings. You will become so familiar with your environment, that if something is different, you will know it immediately.

You may not immediately know exactly what is wrong, but you will know that the situation deserves a second look. You know that more caution is needed.

In this passage, Jesus knew that something was off. He felt *"that virtue had gone out of him"*. In a large, pressing crowd, He knew that someone had touched him. He didn't have to see exactly who it was. He didn't have to know exactly why they were there. He didn't need the details to know that something had changed and He needed to "investigate" further.

Our goal should be to know our surroundings so well that we can tell if something is wrong without having to know the exact details.

Avoidance

"...and he left his garment in her hand, and fled, and got him out."
Genesis 39:12

The ultimate goal of personal security is safety. It is not about winning a fight. It is not about making a point. It is not about beating the other guy. It is not about punishing criminals. It's about keeping you, your friends, and your family safe and secure.

The best way to achieve this goal is to entirely avoid violent conflicts or confrontations. I know that running is not as glorious as victoriously standing on the bad guy's throat, but avoiding conflict will keep you safer and more secure.

If you are never a part of a violent conflict, it is extremely unlikely that you will ever be injured or killed in this non-occurring incident. In fact, there is NO chance. People use statistics to come up with various odds concerning violent encounters, but it's important to remember that these are still odds.

Odds are for betting and you shouldn't bet with the life and health of you and your family members. There is always a chance you could end up on the wrong side of those statistics. You can always lose. The other guy could be tougher, meaner, more committed, or more prepared. Any number of things outside of your control could happen to throw the odds in the favor of your attacker. You could trip or slip. Your eyes could unexpectedly tear up at a chemical or odor. The attacker could have friends just around the corner. You could be suddenly distracted. Violent conflict is an unknown that is not worth exploring.

I am sure that you would not knowingly volunteer to participate in an uncontrolled violent confrontation. But unless you take steps to actively avoid these situations you may be unwittingly maneuvered into a situation where you no longer have a choice in the matter. Let's talk about some of our options for avoiding conflict.

Distance

"And it came to pass, that, as the people pressed upon him to hear the word of God, he stood by the lake of Gennesaret, And saw two ships standing by the lake: but the fishermen were gone out of them, and were washing their nets. And he entered into one of the ships, which was Simon's, and prayed him that he would thrust out a little from the land. And he sat down, and taught the people out of the ship." Luke 5:1-3

Jesus had a large crowd gathering to hear Him speak. These people wanted to hear what He had to say. They probably were not a danger to

47

him. They probably did not intend to harm him in any way, but Jesus was careful. They had backed Him up to a body of water and pressed in close. This situation could have turned very bad very quickly, so Jesus entered a boat and moved out into the water to get some distance from the crowd.

When you go to drivers training, you hear the teachers talk about distancing yourself from the vehicle in front of you. They give you tips like counting several seconds as the leading vehicle passes a landmark to measure your following distance.

This extra distance translates into critical time to react to the unpredictable actions of the vehicle ahead of you. You do not know what they will do. They could slam on the brakes at the sight of a deer. They could have a tire blow out that sends them flying across the road. You don't know what could happen, so you give them space that can create time for you to react.

Keeping your distance from unpredictable individuals is a critical part of maintaining good personal security.

In the same way that distancing your vehicle from another vehicle is good because you don't know what they will do, distancing yourself from unknown individuals is important because you don't know what actions they may take.

There are many factors that should be taken into account when calculating your separation distance. When driving, you have to think about how weather conditions and vehicle weight will affect the time you need to maneuver to safety.

When considering distance in relation to personal security you should similarly ask yourself several questions: How quickly can I flee to a populated area where I can get help? How long would it take for me to draw a defensive tool and ready myself for an attack? How quick are my reflexes? Be realistic and give yourself the necessary amount of space.

Crowds are a double-edged sword. There is some security in the proximity of other human beings. This can deter a logical assailant who considers that these witnesses can harm him or bring him to justice. Unfortunately, logic is not always foremost in the mind of an attacker and a crowd can become just an audience. Although the possibility of resistance can give an attacker pause, there is never any real guarantee that these people around you would come to your aid.

Other times, the crowd itself can be dangerous. When a large group of people are suddenly motivated to act for any reason (fright, greed, etc), it can become very dangerous. We have all heard the stories of people trampled by motivated shoppers on Black Friday or while fleeing a burning building. Those people who were trampled, were trapped and unable to escape the crowd. A nice compromise is to attempt to stay on the outskirts of any large crowd and be ready to get out of the way.

Many people put themselves in close proximity to an assailant out of fear of offending someone. Be careful not to put yourself in danger because of social pressure. If you think it might be dangerous to get on the elevator alone with that person, smile and nod and send the elevator on its way without you. If the person really was a threat, you just saved yourself a lot of trouble. If they were not a threat, they probably forgot about it by the time their ride ended. If someone is walking too close to you, just stop and let them move away. Don't let social pressure put you in situations where you are not comfortable.

I don't expect you to buy a boat and sit in the middle of a lake like Jesus did, but it is definitely a good idea to give yourself the time and space to react to unpredictable behavior.

Departure

"Then took they up stones to cast at him: but Jesus hid himself, and went out of the temple, going through the midst of them, and so passed by."
John 8:59

Here we have angry people getting ready to stone Jesus, but when they went to find their stones, Jesus hid and left the temple.

I can imagine these people getting mad and hurriedly running outside the temple to quickly find a suitably destructive stone to throw at Jesus. These people are motivated and about to assault Jesus. They are looking for blood, but when they return, Jesus is gone. He departed.

He didn't wait until the crowd dispersed. He didn't wait for the police to take reports. He didn't wait around to show off how many angels He could call down from heaven or how well He could fight. He left right then, directly through the crowd.

Sometimes maintaining a safe distance means running away. When an attacker comes after you, departure should be the first option that you consider.

Your first thought should not be, "Can I take him in a fight?" or "How quickly can I draw my gun?" Your first thought should be, "Can I get away? Can I leave this danger behind?" If you have not been keeping a good distance and you don't have the space, time, or wherewithal to immediately get out of danger, your next step is figuring out how you can give yourself the option or ability to depart from that danger zone.

Depart to where? Anywhere safer than your current situation. In the story above, I imagine that Jesus just wanted to be further than a "stone's throw away". He wanted to be in a place where He was out of their reach.

With proper mental preparation and awareness you should have already figured out the best direction to depart. You should have a good idea of where you are running. Don't run down to the end of a pier or dock. Don't run into an unknown dark alley that could be blocked.

Have an escape route in your mind at all times. If something goes wrong where will you go and how will you get there? To your vehicle? The building exit? To the security station? If you are with loved ones, make sure that they know the plan also.

Your ultimate goal in any violent confrontation should be to get to safety.

*And after that many days were fulfilled, the Jews took counsel to kill him:
But their laying await was known of Saul. And they watched the gates day
and night to kill him. Then the disciples took him by night, and let him
down by the wall in a basket. Acts 9:23-25*

We have Saul in a similar situation here with an interesting twist. There
are people waiting at the gates of the city to kill him. They are trying to
block his departure. They are trying to keep him from escaping, but Saul
gets creative and finds a way out. He has his friends lower him over the
wall in a basket.

Even when departure was made difficult and nigh unto impossible, Saul
still saw it as his first option. Escaping over the wall was no easy
proposition. We are not talking about the eight foot wall that surrounds
my house. We are talking about a massive wall that defended the entire
city. This wall was purposefully built to be difficult and dangerous to get
over.

Even though Saul knew his enemies' plans, the enemies still waited by the
gates because they knew the danger and difficulty of trying to escape a
different way. Saul had to put his life into the hands of others during the
dangerous act of lowering him over the wall in order to escape. One slip
of the rope could drop him and break his neck. He was completely
vulnerable in that basket with no recourse if he or his helpers were
attacked.

We are talking about a man who, not long before this, was simply killing
those who did not agree with him, yet here he has no ego problem putting
his life in the hands of others to lower him over the wall and escape his
enemies. He realized that departure, however difficult in this case, was a
better option than a confrontation with his zealously murderous enemies.

Never underestimate the value and effectiveness of a sudden departure.

De-escalation

"Now Moses in the law commanded us, that such should be stoned: but what sayest thou? This they said, tempting him, that they might have to accuse him. But Jesus stooped down, and with his finger wrote on the ground, as though he heard them not. So when they continued asking him, he lifted up himself, and said unto them, He that is without sin among you, let him first cast a stone at her. And again he stooped down, and wrote on the ground. And they which heard it, being convicted by their own conscience, went out one by one, beginning at the eldest, even unto the last: and Jesus was left alone, and the woman standing in the midst."
John 8:5-9

We have men here who brought to Jesus a woman that they were about to kill. It is just my opinion, but based on Jesus' words, I believe that they

53

already had the stones in their hands. They were ready to kill. Jesus didn't say, "He that is without sin among you, let him first go and get a stone and cast it at her." The understanding was that they were ready to kill her and they were hoping that they could include Jesus in this stoning. Two for the price of one. They wanted to trick Jesus so that they could accuse Him and kill Him too. This wasn't the first time that people had been trying to kill Jesus.

Jesus takes a different course of action than in the previous story (which actually happens later in this chapter). He does not run away in this case. He decides to make them go away and he doesn't have to use violence. He does it with words. He used his finger to write on the ground.

The words that Jesus wrote on the ground caused these men to change their mind. They no longer thought it was a good idea to murder the woman, let alone Jesus. The bloodthirsty Pharisees all left one by one until only Jesus and the woman were left and were no longer in danger of being stoned. This is the perfect example of de-escalation.

De-escalation is "a reduction in intensity" (of a crisis or a war). With de-escalation, our goal is to lower tensions, risks, and danger. We want to de-escalate a situation to keep someone from actually carrying out an act of violence. We want to remove the risk and danger without coming to bullets or blows.

When we discussed awareness, we talked about the warning signs that precede many violent confrontations. When we spot these warning signs, we may have the option of de-escalating the situation. It's not always an option, but a successful de-escalation is always better than a violent encounter with an unknown outcome.

Wait a second! Didn't I just say that departure should be our first consideration? Yes, but there are several good reasons for you to de-escalate a dangerous situation.

First, you might need to de-escalate the situation because you are not able to run. Maybe you are surrounded or cornered. Maybe you are not physically fit enough to escape the danger. Maybe you have a family with you and you are not certain that they are quick enough to escape the danger. If you cannot escape the danger, try to remove it through de-escalation.

Maybe you don't want to depart because it would be expensive, difficult, or wasteful to leave immediately and you aren't willing to give up what you have invested to get to this point. In some cases, the task or mission that you are trying to accomplish is worth the added risk of sticking around and attempting to de-escalate the situation.

You may be looking to the future and trying to pave the way for future encounters. Maybe you care about the person who is endangering you and you sincerely want to help them. There are any number of reasons why you might attempt to de-escalate the situation before departing.

Different personalities and people with different motivations require different de-escalation methods. You should first try to figure out the reasoning behind their actions. Do they want money? Do they want revenge? Do they want to hurt someone?

People with different goals will be motivated, and in our case, demotivated in different ways. If a thief only wants money, then convincing them that you don't have anything of value might de-escalate the situation and cause them to leave you alone. If someone is looking for revenge, the same tact probably would not work. You might want to remind them of the consequences of their intended actions. You might want to scare the living daylights out of them. Reason, fear, compassion, and more can all be used in your attempts to de-escalate a dangerous situation.

The Bible says that the enemies of Jesus left "one by one, beginning with the eldest..." If you are dealing with a threat from a group, be sure to speak to an individual. You aren't trying to convince a group, you are trying to convince one individual at a time. Focus on one person and try to motivate that one person to leave or give up.

Start with a leader like Jesus did. The eldest was the first to leave and the others followed. Do whatever you can to convince that leader that a violent confrontation is not in their best interest. Tell them how it will not accomplish their goals. If you convince the leader first, it will normally be easier to convince the others afterward.

Remember that de-escalation doesn't always work. People don't always listen to reason. You should still have a backup plan. You should be evaluating your efforts as you are speaking. If you see that your attempts at de-escalation are not working, know when to cut your losses and move on to Plan B.

Discretion

Then asked he them again, Whom seek ye? And they said, Jesus of Nazareth. Jesus answered, I have told you that I am he: if therefore ye seek me, let these go their way: That the saying might be fulfilled, which he spake, Of them which thou gavest me have I lost none. Then Simon Peter having a sword drew it, and smote the high priest's servant, and cut off his right ear. The servant's name was Malchus. Then said Jesus unto Peter, Put up thy sword into the sheath: the cup which my Father hath given me, shall I not drink it? John 18:7-11

The soldiers, chief priests, and Pharisees came to take Jesus away. We can see several verses earlier that Jesus knew exactly what was happening and actually approached these men Himself. This encounter would eventually lead to His death, but Jesus knew this. This death was the ultimate reason that He came to earth. This encounter was an essential part of His plan.

These men weren't any "danger" to Jesus in the sense that they did not hurt His purpose or plan. But Simon Peter had a sword and decided to use it. Having the sword was not the problem. Jesus had previously inquired to make sure that they had a sword. He was glad that they had a sword. The problem was that Simon Peter did not need to use the sword at that moment.

Jesus was asking his enemies to allow His disciples to go free. They had not refused. Things were still going well. There was no trouble yet, but Simon Peter decided to draw his sword and take matters into his own hands.

Take a moment and think about how the ear of the servant of the high priest could have been cut off. The ear is pretty integral to the whole "head thing" on top of your shoulders. It is very likely that Peter was trying to take the man's head off with the sword. When the man twisted his head sideways, Simon Peter barely missed and ended up severing the servant's ear instead of his neck.

Talk about overreacting! These men came seeking Jesus, and while He was still talking to them, Peter drew his sword and tried to take a man's head off.

We can scoff at Peter and smile about the story because Jesus managed to de-escalate the situation and reattach the man's ear, but Peter's overreaction and lack of discretion are actually rather common, even today.

People often take offense or get worked up over unimportant matters. Does it really matter what a complete stranger says about your mother? Why do you care about the hand gesture that another driver decided to share with you? Just let it go. Use some discretion.

Don't get carried away when there is no real danger. Don't jump into conflict over unimportant matters. This is what happened to Peter.

The previous three avoidance techniques: keeping your distance, de-escalating, and running away are all physical acts that can be seen, yet they are all easier than this final, most important mental aspect of avoidance.

It is much easier to talk about using discretion than to actually accomplish it. It's about *self*-control and *self*-control can be far more difficult than controlling a wild animal. Our minds are funny things. In the heat of the moment, it's hard to back down from a perceived challenge. It is tough to de-escalate your own mind.

Before you decide to take part in a violent confrontation, ask yourself, "Is this worth losing my life? Is this worth ending up in jail? Is this worth losing my home to pay someone's medical expenses?" The answer might be yes. There are a few things that are more important than your personal life and property, but you need to be aware of the risk involved before joining that fight.

Who goes into a real fight believing that they will lose? Everyone thinks they will come out on the other side as the victor. "Who cares about the consequences of losing! They don't apply to me because I won't lose."

They apply to everyone. Losing a fight is always a possibility. I know it's tough to convince your ego, but better men than yourself have lost fights for unexpected and seemingly trivial reasons.

Self-control and discretion can keep you from participating in unnecessary conflict and exposing yourself to unnecessary risk.

Deception

And the lords of the Philistines came up unto her, and said unto her, Entice him, and see wherein his great strength lieth, and by what means we may prevail against him, that we may bind him to afflict him: and we will give thee every one of us eleven hundred pieces of silver. And Delilah said to Samson, Tell me, I pray thee, wherein thy great strength lieth, and wherewith thou mightest be bound to afflict thee. And Samson said unto her, If they bind me with seven green withs that were never dried, then shall I be weak, and be as another man. Then the lords of the Philistines brought up to her seven green withs which had not been dried, and she bound him with them. Now there were men lying in wait, abiding with her in the chamber. And she said unto him, The Philistines be upon thee, Samson. And he brake the withs, as a thread of tow is broken when it toucheth the fire. So his strength was not known. And Delilah said unto Samson, Behold, thou hast mocked me, and told me lies: now tell me, I pray thee, wherewith thou mightest be bound. Judges 16:5-10

Samson's enemies were using someone that he loved to find out the secret of his strength. Once they found this secret, they wanted to take away his strength and capture him. The source of Samson's strength was a great mystery to his enemies and he was smart to keep it that way. When Samson gave up the secret, it was used against him. He was taken into captivity and his eyes were gouged out.

Sometimes good personal security means keeping secrets from those that may not have your best interests in mind.

For some people this can be very difficult. They are perfectly willing to talk about anything and everything. Their life is an open book. They are helpful, kind souls and will share any information with anyone that asks. They want to show off their tools and talk about their skills and tactics. Unfortunately, this attitude can be very dangerous.

There are reasons that an army doesn't broadcast how much firepower they have at their disposal. If they are very weak, they don't want the enemy to know that now is the time to attack. If they are very strong, they want the element of surprise. It is important to keep information from your enemies.

There are times when you want to be overestimated. You do not want to appear weak. You may want a criminal to think you are more dangerous than you really are so that they don't select you as a victim.

Every criminal has a victim selection process. This process factors in the information that they think they know about you. Do they think you look unfamiliar with your surroundings? Do they think you look weak and unsure of yourself? Does it look like you are not paying attention to your surroundings? You may look like the perfect victim.

In an unfamiliar or dangerous neighborhood, it might be a good idea to walk at a brisk pace and look like you know where you are going and what you are doing. Even if you don't know exactly where you are or what you are doing, it is probably a good idea to pretend like you do. You are manipulating their perception so that they don't see you as an opportune victim. You are deceiving them. In a way, this could be considered an attempt at de-escalation. You are trying to use their perception and logic to convince them that an attack is not a good idea.

If you happen to be selected as a victim, you are done trying to convince them that they made a mistake. They have already decided to assault, attack, or rob you. Now you need to let them think you are the most passive, docile, purring kitty that they have ever encountered. Get their guard down. Do not let them suspect anything. Your acting should be so good that their jaws should be stuck on the floor when you get in that killer sucker punch/kick or pull out your concealed weapon.

Shock and surprise are amazing force multipliers. One single blow with shock and surprise can often have the same effect as five bloody minutes worth of trading punches. Your deception is what gives you this advantage.

Concealed carry and open carry are two extremely different approaches to carrying a defensive weapon and both can be used effectively. Both carry methods have their advantages and disadvantages. My personal preference is to keep a defensive weapon a secret. I'd like for it to be my ace in the hole. Most people would argue that openly carrying a defensive weapon will keep you from being selected as a victim, but it can be very difficult to shock and surprise someone while openly carrying.

The important part is knowing how to make the most of whatever tact you take. Know the advantages of each option and make them work for you. Wherever possible, control the information that others know about. You can use that information to tell a story that will give you the upper hand in a dangerous situation.

Conflict

Wouldn't it be wonderful if we could entirely avoid conflict? Wouldn't it be great if we never had to progress past our avoidance techniques? Absolutely! But unfortunately, there are people that cannot be reasoned with. There are traps from which we cannot escape. There are situations where conflict is unavoidable. We all hope that it won't happen to us, but there is no magic talisman that can guarantee that it won't.

By the time you actually get to a violent encounter, there is very little to decide and do. Do what you have already decided to do. Use the skills you have honed during training. Use the gear that you already selected and should have on hand.

There are, however, a few critical aspects of any conflict that cannot be forgotten. Not everything can be done in advance. There are two things to remember that are absolutely critical if you expect to succeed in and survive a violent conflict.

We have all heard some variation of the age-old coaching advice, "Give it your all, and play till the buzzer." When you are in a fight for your life, the same principles apply. Don't hold back and don't quit. Commit and continue.

Commit

"For God so loved the world, that he gave his only begotten Son, that whosoever believeth in him should not perish, but have everlasting life."
John 3:16

The most powerful story in all of the Bible is the story of Jesus Christ willingly giving His own life on Calvary's cross. Why? It is because He made the *ultimate* sacrifice. This story is powerful because the Lord Jesus Christ saw a great need, and completely committed himself to remedying the problem even when it required His life.

In a society full of people accustomed to half-hearted effort, complete commitment can be as difficult to find as .380 brass in three-foot high grass. Most people are only willing to put in an allotted amount of effort and if that doesn't work, they quit. This approach won't work if you hope to survive a violent confrontation.

Jesus saw a critical need that had to be dealt with. He saw souls that would perish without His action. He saw individuals in need. He saw a situation that He could not leave alone and He did something about it. When He saw the peril of our souls, He didn't hold back. He didn't draw the line and say, "I'll do this much." He committed entirely. He went all out. He gave His life.

If you are in a violent conflict, you have seen or encountered a great need. You or someone you care about is in grave danger. You have reached a point where conflict is the only option.

If you followed the advice in previous chapters, you are not fighting for a dumb cause. This isn't about a "yo-mama" insult. This conflict is serious and necessary. You don't have to worry about second thoughts. You have already thought this out in advance and made the decisions that led you here.

Now you need to do whatever it takes to eliminate the threat or danger. You need to commit whatever resources are necessary. You need to commit whatever energy is necessary. You need to commit to whatever violence is necessary.

Humans are capable of amazingly potent and devastating violence, but this animalistic behaviour is mostly suppressed, and with good reason. In a "civilized" society, our violent instincts are rarely called upon. But when they are needed, it's important that we let them take center stage with no shackles or leg-irons to hold them back. If the conflict requires violence, commit to providing whatever is necessary to remove yourself or your loved ones from harm.

If you have something worth fighting for, don't hold back.

"Whatsoever thy hand findeth to do, do it with thy might; for there is no work, nor device, nor knowledge, nor wisdom, in the grave, whither thou goest." Ecclesiastes 9:10

I pray that you will never have to lose someone dear or something precious and later wonder if there was more that you could have done. If you fully commit during the conflict, you will never have to look back from a hospital bed or the graveside of a loved one and ask those questions. You will know that no matter the outcome, you were fully committed to the conflict.

Continue

"But the Egyptians pursued after them, all the horses and chariots of Pharaoh, and his horsemen, and his army, and overtook them encamping by the sea, beside Pihahiroth, before Baalzephon. And when Pharaoh drew nigh, the children of Israel lifted up their eyes, and, behold, the Egyptians marched after them; and they were sore afraid: and the children of Israel cried out unto the LORD. And they said unto Moses, Because there were no graves in Egypt, hast thou taken us away to die in the wilderness? wherefore hast thou dealt thus with us, to carry us forth out of Egypt? Is not this the word that we did tell thee in Egypt, saying, Let us alone, that we may serve the Egyptians? For it had been better for us to serve the Egyptians, than that we should die in the wilderness."
Exodus 14:9-12

The children of Israel have finally escaped from the oppression of the Egyptians and are headed to the Promised Land, but now with a little perceived adversity they are ready to give up and head back into the danger that they so recently escaped. From our armchair-quarterback position, we see how ridiculous this is, yet the Israelites who faced this seemingly insurmountable obstacle found it to be a completely viable option.

When it comes to conflict (with the safety of you or your loved ones on the line), you absolutely cannot quit. Allowing the threat to come to fruition is not a viable option. No matter how difficult, scary, or impossible the task, you cannot quit.

Conflict is rarely simple or straightforward. It's not like the movies where you see the good guys win easily and their scratches all disappear by the next scene. It hurts, destroys, and maims. It is bloody and scary. For these very reasons, we should do everything possible to avoid it, but when it is forced upon us, we cannot let the unpleasant realities of conflict deter us from accomplishing a necessary goal.

Conflict is the inevitable result of two opposing goals. Your goal is the safety and security of you and your family. The assailant's goal is to harm or rob you. These two goals cannot coexist. Only one of you can achieve your goal. Thus conflict ensues.

Never enter a conflict without a specific goal and never stop fighting until that goal has been accomplished. Without a goal, you will never "win". How would you even know if you won? Without a goal, you lose every time.

This is not to say that every conflict has to end with a dead, maimed, beaten down, or incarcerated opponent, but you must have a specific goal in mind and not quit until that goal has been accomplished.

Your overall goal should be to get to a place of safety or to remove the immediate danger, but you still need to get more detailed than that. Decide what would be a successful outcome. In your specific situation, it might mean creating a distraction or diversion that allows your family to escape. It might mean drawing enough attention that the attacker has to disengage and leave you alone. It might mean getting past your opponent and escaping. There can be several positive possible outcomes, but you should have a well-defined goal and continue until you achieve your goal!

Conclusion

The concepts covered in this book are both simple and critical. Many intelligent people will read through this book, get to the conclusion, and say, "Of course! Now that you mention it, that makes sense." There might even be an impulse to dismiss such simplistic advice, but simple shouldn't be mistaken for inconsequential.

The goal of this book is not to wow you with my mental prowess (as if that's possible), but to provide realistic and practical advice that can make you safer.

Prepare. Be aware. Avoid conflict. Fight with everything you have till you reach safety. So simple, yet I still wonder how much will be absorbed and applied.

Just reading this book won't make you safer. That requires action on your part: decisions, changes in mindset. These concepts are useless if they remain only as theories on paper or in your mind. They must be put to use.

Don't delay their implementation. None of the actions in this book require great sums of money, exorbitant amounts of time, or ninja-like skills. You can't use those excuses.

I challenge you to immediately sit down with a pen and paper and make a list of actions that you can take today and decisions that you can make right now.

If this book helps you to find one area and take even just one step toward increasing your safety and security, I will consider this book a success.

Take care and God bless.

Please take a moment to review this book for myself and others:

You can use this link:
http://amzn.to/tacticalbiblestoriesreview

Or search amazon.com for "Tactical Bible Stories" and click on the yellow "Write a Customer Review" button.

Thank you!

About the Author

Rob Robideau is a husband and father, preacher, self-defense web show host, pilot, writer, and more. He currently resides in an upscale village south of Kathmandu, Nepal.

This book is based on his personal experience while living with his family in a "least developed country" with an unstable government. He has also incorporated what he has learned from numerous hours spent with individuals who have been studying, teaching, and writing about the dynamics of interpersonal conflict for many years.

Made in the USA
San Bernardino, CA
11 November 2015